I would like to dedicate this book to
all the parents, teachers and extended family
who help us become the best version of ourselves.

Acknowledgements: To Ray for bringing such joy into my life.
To Larry for your incredible talent. To Chick for bringing the characters
to life with your amazing gift of color. Thank you all so very much.

It's sunny and bright

As she helps Trainer Tim
with their trip to the beach

Randy is laughing

And Tammy is shouting

While all the time helping
prepare for the outing

Trainer Tim checks his list,
in all the commotion.
Beach towels, aloe vera and
plenty of suntan lotion

Packed are the shovels
and bright colored pails

The camera and binocculars in hopes of seeing some whales!

Umbrellas, blankets
toys for the sand

Our castles and sculptures will truly be grand

The kids are all squealing
Hurry! Hurry!

As we start down the road
to our long day's journey

We search the coast

For just the right spot

And there are smiles galore
as we park in the lot

Okay, Everyone
Before we go in we must
apply sunblock
to protect our skin

Everybody line up
We'll start with the nose

Then ears,
Both shoulders

And down to the...toes?

Now we are ready

Let's all jump in

Bobby grabs the snorkel

The mask

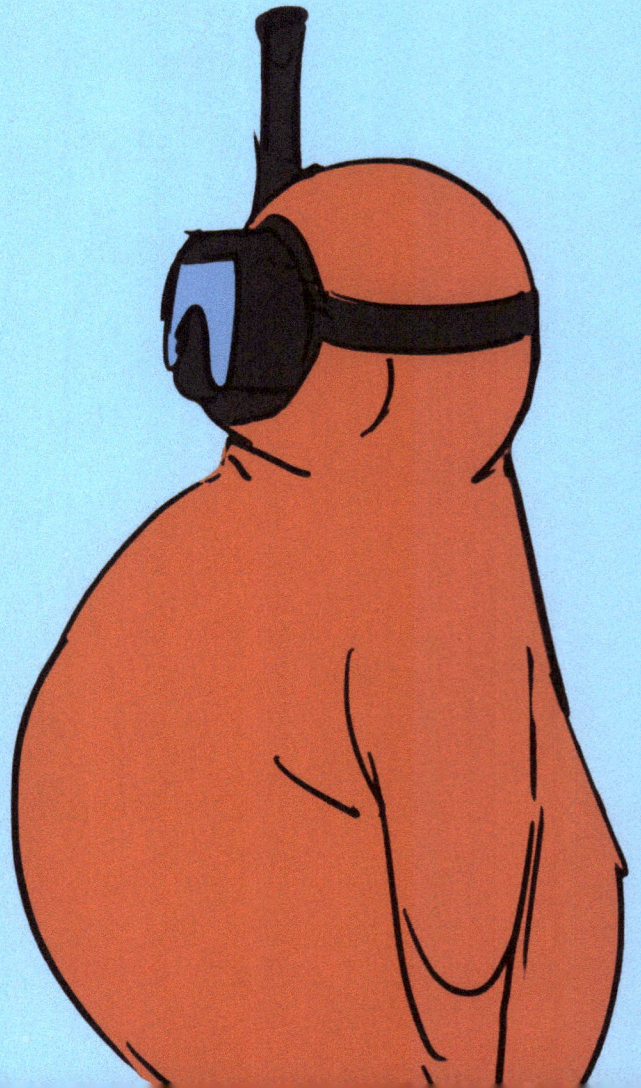

And fins...

Susie is timid
but Freddy is brave

To catch the next wave

Olivia is searching for
sea shells
that the tide washed in

Tammy builds castles assisted by Trainer Tim

Let's all play a game
of volleyball!

A day at the beach
is so full of fun

Before you know it
down goes the sun

Let's collect everything up
and end with a song

And a stroll down the path
merrily along

One last thing
I would like to say
Thank you for coming to
the beach with me today!

Trainer Tim's Tips for a Healthier You

Trainer Tim's At the Beach

Going to the beach is great fun,
especially when you are going with friends

Be a good helper and help pack the car as well
as unpacking the car when you get to the beach

Carrying your towel and sand toys to the beach
is a great help as well

Make sure that you always have sunblock on and
wear a hat when you are not in the water

Always pick up any trash or bottles that you see,
and put them in the garbage

Never go in the ocean alone,
always make sure you have an adult with you

Always share your sand toys with others
and that will help you make new friends

Tim Green
"Trainer Tim"

Tim Green grew up in Ohio where his parents instilled the belief, "Everything is possible for those who work hard". He has worked with dozens of celebrities, (Richard Simmons, Kathy Ireland, Paula Abdul, Jody Foster) and contributes to most of the leading magazines, including Self, Shape and Fit, Pregnancy. He was the fitness editor of Golf Magazine and the resident fitness director for the hit show "90210".

Tim's ongoing experience working with children's organizations and his work with kids from the inner city to the wealthiest communities has led him to believe that the common need all children have is to be loved and nurtured

He has created a character called "Trainer Tim". As this character, he tells children how their health and fitness affects their bodies, schoolwork, playtime and, in fact, their entire lives. His positive influence builds their self-esteem, elevates their motivation and helps them improve their overall health. Reading the books of"Trainer Tim" will certainly touch the kid in all of us.

www.ingramcontent.com/pod-product-compliance
Lightning Source LLC
Chambersburg PA
CBHW040303100426
42811CB00011B/1348